Welcome to the American Revolution Museum at Yorktown®

The American Revolution Museum at Yorktown offers a national perspective on the struggle for independence of 13 British American Colonies and tells compelling stories of real people who played a role in the creation of the United States. Located in America's Historic Triangle and adjacent to the Yorktown Battlefield where American independence was won, the museum offers experiences for all members of the family.

Originally opening in 1976 as the Yorktown Victory Center, the 80,000-square-foot American Revolution Museum at Yorktown debuted in April 2017 and features immersive museum galleries, engaging films and expanded living-history programs in a re-created Continental Army encampment and Revolution-era farm.

"Freedom's Sentinel," depicts an eagle enveloping two eaglets between its outspread wings. A stars-and-stripes shield on the eagle's chest represents the 13 Colonies at the time of the Revolution, and the two eaglets reflect the museum's mission to educate future generations. The 18-foot-wide, 500-pound sculpture hangs on the pediment above the museum entrance.

TIPS FOR TOURING

Getting Started

★ Allow at least three to four hours to visit the American Revolution Museum at Yorktown.

★ All areas of the museum are wheelchair accessible. Strollers, wheelchairs and motorized scooters are available in the lobby on a first-come, first-served basis. Service animals are welcome throughout the museum exhibits. All films are open-captioned.

★ There are timed programs and demonstrations throughout the day. Ask staff for details.

★ Look out for special exhibitions in our changing exhibition gallery.

★ Enjoy *Liberty Fever,* an 18-minute introductory film shown throughout the day in our 170-seat theater.

★ While visiting our 22,000-square-foot American Revolution galleries, create an embossed stamp on your map similar to ones used during the Stamp Act crisis.

★ Play our Battle Game, and leave a message on our Liberty Tree. Look for locations where you can take photos in the galleries.

★ Witness *The Siege of Yorktown* in our experiential theater, located in the American Revolution galleries. Thrill to the sounds, smells and drama of the most decisive battle of the war during this eight-minute presentation.

★ Outdoors, stop by the transitional pavilion to find out the day's activities in the living-history areas. This is a great spot for a family photo.

★ Watch demonstrations of daily life and talk to historical interpreters in the re-created Continental Army encampment and Revolution-era farm.

★ Refuel at the museum's café.

★ Take something home from the gift shop to remember your visit.

A marble statue symbolizing the great military victory at Yorktown in 1781, stands in Victory Hall. It was a gift of the late Nick and Mary Mathews, who donated the land upon which the museum stands and who supported museum programs during their lifetimes and through their estate. This replica of "Winged Victory of Samothrace" depicts Nike, Greek goddess of victory.

2 ✦ *Jamestown-Yorktown Foundation*

TIPS FOR TOURING

Talk to Interpreters

After touring the American Revolution galleries, step outside and visit the re-created Continental Army encampment and Revolution-era farm, where you can see, hear, smell and touch everyday life during the Revolution.

Historical interpreters, dressed in period attire, are there to offer informative and interactive demonstrations. These professional museum educators will speak to you in 21st-century language that allows them to trace changes through time and make connections between the historic events of the American Revolution and today.

We encourage you to talk with them, ask questions, try activities, participate in hands-on demonstrations and take photos. Activities and demonstrations vary from season to season.

American Revolution Museum at Yorktown ✦ 3

YORKTOWN

The Colonial Town of York

*I*n October 1781, American and French troops descended on Yorktown, Virginia, to lay siege on the army of British General Charles Cornwallis. The ensuing battle would change the course of history.

Situated on a deep navigable river of the same name, the Virginia General Assembly established York in 1691. By the 1740s, it was one of the most important centers of trade and shipping in Virginia. From here, merchants exported large quantities of tobacco and other commodities while importing cargoes of English and European-made goods. The town also became the main entry for many enslaved people from Africa and the West Indies who worked in the tobacco fields of Virginia.

By the 1770s, other ports such as Norfolk had surpassed Yorktown, but it was still a busy trading center with more than 250 buildings and nearly 1,800 inhabitants. The siege of 1781 destroyed more than half of the town's buildings, and it never regained its earlier commercial importance.

Today, Yorktown is known for its waterfront charm, 18th-century architecture, historic battlefield and colonial history. Yorktown is one of three sites making up America's Historic Triangle, which also includes Jamestown and Williamsburg.

VIEW OF THE TOWN OF YORK, by John Gauntlett, 1755.
Courtesy of The Mariners' Museum, Newport News, Virginia

"There are about 10 good Houses, not above 4 of Brick, the rest of Timber viz. Pine Planks Covered with Shingles of Cypress ... Here is a neat Stone Church with a bell & they are Just finishing a Court house or Town hall of Brick with a Piazza before it, very handsom & convenient."

– WILLIAM GROVE, 1732

INTRODUCTORY FILM

Liberty Fever

Set 25 years after the events of the American Revolution, an early 1800s storyteller shares accounts of the war using a moving panorama, or "crankie." The storyteller's performance is interwoven with live-action film segments featuring the real stories of five people who lived during the American Revolution.

George Hewes witnessed the Boston Massacre in 1770. Billy Flora was a hero of the Battle of Great Bridge in Virginia in 1775. Isabella Ferguson was an Irish immigrant to South Carolina and a strong supporter of the Patriot cause. John Howland, a young Continental Army soldier, witnessed the Battle of Princeton. Peter Harris, a Catawba Indian from South Carolina, fought on the American side. Watch the spread of liberty fever as their stories unfold.

WHAT'S A CRANKIE?

This late 1700s and early 1800s form of mass media was popular with people of all ages. It was an apparatus with a long roll of paper on which dramatic backlit silhouettes scrolled in front of the audience. Some crankies were huge and were shown in theaters and exhibition halls, while others were much smaller and portable to travel throughout the countryside.

AMERICAN REVOLUTION GALLERIES

Top 10 Artifacts

1. King George III portrait
2. Ayuba Suleiman Diallo portrait
3. Early American long rifle
4. Portable lap desk
5. Declaration of Independence

THE NEW NATION

THE AMERICAN PEOPLE

AMERICAN REVOLUTION TIMELINE

Media

- **A** "British Colonial America in 1763" interactive
- **B** *Changing Relationships* film
- **C** *Saratoga: First Great Victory* film
- **D** *Print Shop* video
- **E** "Personal Stories of the Revolution" interactive
- **F** "Battles of the American Revolution" interactive
- **G** Battle Game
- **H** *Siege of Yorktown* experiential theater
- **I** "Constitution" interactive
- **J** *U.S. Constitution and the Bill of Rights* film
- **K** "Liberty Tree" interactive
- **L** "Migration and the First Census" interactive map

6 ★ *Jamestown-Yorktown Foundation*

AMERICAN REVOLUTION GALLERIES

6 Sword from the court of Louis XVI
7 Daniel Morgan miniature portrait
8 Wedgewood anti-slavery medallion
9 Statue of George Washington
10 Brownsville, Pennsylvania ferry marker

1 *Oil on canvas coronation portrait of King George III by the studio of Allan Ramsay, Principal Painter in Ordinary at the royal court, circa 1762-84.*

AMERICAN REVOLUTION GALLERIES

British Colonial America

In 1750, 26 years before the Declaration of Independence, Britain's American colonies stretched from Canada to the Caribbean. The 13 Colonies that would become the United States were only part of Britain's vast empire. King George III had supreme authority over these territories and appointed a royal governor in most colonies to represent him. Each colony typically had its own legislative assembly, elected by property owning male residents only.

It soon became apparent there were limits to the power of a king and his ministers 4,000 miles away. Colonial assemblies resisted attempts to enforce royal policies with which they disagreed. By 1750, the assemblies had established the right to approve certain appointments, pass laws and levy taxes. Increasingly, they came to think of themselves as minor parliaments—subject to the king but with their own local power.

★ ★ ★

The People of British North America

By 1750, more than two million people lived in the 13 Colonies and represented several dozen cultural and religious traditions. The greatest single ethnic and cultural change in the colonies was the forced immigration of hundreds of thousands of enslaved Africans. Africans and African Americans constituted 25 percent of the people living in the colonies, and in South Carolina and Georgia, their number was greater than those of English or European descent.

The transatlantic slave trade is well documented. The personal lives of its victims are not. An exception is Ayuba Suleiman Diallo, a Fulani Muslim merchant and scholar from Senegambia in Africa. Seized and sold by his enemies, he arrived in Annapolis, Maryland, and was enslaved on a tobacco plantation in 1731. Diallo drew the attention of a lawyer who secured his freedom and sailed with him to England. There he won the respect of leading intellectuals and ultimately entered the annals of history as a figure embraced by the global abolitionist movement. He was so famous he had his portrait painted in England. Diallo eventually returned to Africa.

AYUBA SULEIMAN DIALLO, *one of two rare 1730s portraits by William Hoare. Diallo insisted he "be drawn in his own Country Dress" rather than in European clothing.*

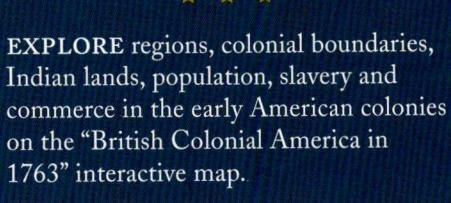

★ ★ ★

EXPLORE regions, colonial boundaries, Indian lands, population, slavery and commerce in the early American colonies on the "British Colonial America in 1763" interactive map.

American Revolution Museum at Yorktown 9

AMERICAN REVOLUTION GALLERIES

The War That Changed Everything

Beginning in the 1600s, Great Britain and France competed to dominate lands in America. By 1754, skirmishing in the Ohio territory led to all-out war. Known as the French and Indian War (1754-1763) in North America and the Seven Years' War in Europe, the fighting soon spread to Europe, the Caribbean, the Mediterranean and even to India.

By 1763, the British had defeated the French on land and sea, but the war left Britain deeply in debt and determined to raise taxes on the American colonies to pay for their defense. This soon would lead to a growing disagreement between the British and the Americans over their respective roles within the empire.

JABEZ HALL POWDER HORN, *engraved with the date "5 Sept 1757" and "Lieutenant Jabez Hall." Hall served with the 2nd and 3rd Connecticut Regiments in the French and Indian War. Militiamen often decorated their powder horns with carved names, slogans and military scenes.*

EARLY AMERICAN LONG RIFLE, *probably Virginia, circa 1750. Known as the long rifle, this form of firearm evolved in America in the early 1700s and became the iconic firearm of the American frontier.*

Moving West and Indians in British Colonial America

Each British colony included substantial Indian populations. Indians living along the Atlantic seaboard had lost most of their ancestral lands and were under British control. Even those living apart from the settlers in separate tribal communities had to accept the authority of the King. Farther west, however, large politically independent Indian groups still held territories claimed, but not actually controlled, by Britain.

The relationship between Indian groups and individual settlers was complex. Some colonists interacted peacefully with the Indians and carried on a profitable trade with them, while others wanted to seize Indian lands for themselves. To the great disappointment of Virginia and Pennsylvania land speculators who had fought in the French and Indian War (including George Washington), King George III issued the Proclamation of 1763 barring settlement beyond the Appalachian Mountains. The British government wanted no more expensive Indian wars.

In short, land west of the line could not be surveyed, leased or purchased. British colonists quickly came to resent this restrictive policy.

BEAR GORGET, *American, late 1750–1775. Military officers in the 1700s wore gorgets around their necks as a sign of rank. This brass and silver gorget probably was made for presentation to an Iroquois Indian leader. The design may have appealed to the Mohawk people, because the bear was a valued symbol to them.*

SEMICIRCUMFERENTOR, *made by Daniel King, Massachusetts, circa 1758. This inexpensively made American instrument is an example of those used for surveying frontier lands.*

proclamation 1763

And We do hereby strictly forbid, on Pain of our Displeasure, all our loving Subjects from making any Purchases or Settlements whatever…

AMERICAN REVOLUTION GALLERIES

British North America and British Economy

For more than a century, the British government controlled colonial American trade through the Navigation Acts. These laws prevented the American colonies from trading directly with other nations. Colonial exports had to travel across the Atlantic in British ships.

Britain relied on her American colonies for agricultural products such as tobacco and indigo, while the colonies were important consumers of British manufactured goods such as clothing, tools, housewares and most other finished products. Enterprises that challenged this model were strongly discouraged.

Through taxes and regulations, Britain attempted to force the American colonial economy into a pattern that would benefit the mother country and the empire as a whole.

PUNCHBOWL, *made of English tin-glazed earthenware, circa 1766. The interior inscription, "Success to Trade," represented the sentiments of many gathered around to enjoy the popular drink in this punchbowl.*

Merchants established stores where Virginians could buy all manner of imported goods manufactured in Britain.

Statue of Virginian Patrick Henry

Patrick Henry, as a member of the Virginia House of Burgesses, championed resistance to the Stamp Act. Ten years later in March 1775 at St. John's Church in Richmond, Virginia, he raised a rallying cry for those Americans disenchanted with British rule: "…but as for me, give me Liberty or give me death!" Patrick Henry's zeal and eloquence made him the prophet for the cause of the American Revolution.

★ ★ ★

MAKE YOUR OWN STAMP. Insert your museum guide into the embosser, press down firmly on the lever, release and slide your stamped paper out of the embosser. Feel the raised image of the stamp.

Britain Moves to Tax and Control

After the Seven Years' War, Britain was determined to tighten its control of the colonies and make them pay a larger share of the costs of defense and imperial government. An early result of this new policy was the Sugar Act of 1764, which included new enforcement provisions to combat widespread smuggling. Customs officials could search warehouses for smuggled goods using vague search warrants, and British judges, instead of local juries, would try defendants.

In 1765, Parliament passed the Stamp Act, imposing a direct tax on most publications, legal documents and licenses. A stamp pressed, or embossed, on the paper proved the tax had been paid. This new tax applied to all residents in every colony. Following Virginia's lead, opposition to the measure became widespread and often violent, making it impossible to enforce. Colonists protested that Parliament had no right to impose a direct internal tax on the colonists; this was the right of their colonial assemblies. Responding to pressure from British merchants, Parliament repealed the law in 1766, but reaffirmed its right to tax the colonists.

AMERICAN REVOLUTION GALLERIES

The Crisis Deepens

Parliament in Britain became increasingly determined to assert its authority, and the colonists were equally determined to defend what they saw as their inherited rights as "Englishmen." In 1767, the Townshend Acts created indirect, external taxes on British goods imported to America. The colonists resisted by boycotting British goods. Once again, Parliament had to withdraw the duties, except for the tax on tea.

The struggle between Britain and its American colonies grew beyond taxation to include control over most colonial affairs. In 1773, Boston Patriots disguised as Indians dumped a valuable cargo of tea into the harbor. To punish Massachusetts, an angry Parliament passed a series of laws that included closing the port of Boston, limiting self-government and other rights, and quartering British soldiers. Colonists saw these "Intolerable Acts" as a threat to the liberties of all British America.

Yorktown Tea Party

In Virginia, most merchants agreed to stop imports, but in November 1774, a ship called *Virginia* arrived in Yorktown from England, carrying two half-chests of tea. The tea had been imported for the merchant John Prentis of Williamsburg. On the morning of November 7, some Yorktown citizens boarded the ship and threw it in the river. This Yorktown tea party forced John Prentis to print an apology in *The Virginia Gazette*.

SILVER PICTURE-BACK SPOON, *one of a set made by T. Tookey of London in 1773. Inscribed with "I love liberty," this spoon represented the sentiments of Englishmen on both sides of the Atlantic.*

Boston Massacre, a scene from *Liberty Fever*

By 1770, mobs in Boston increasingly harassed customs officials and British troops assigned to protect them. On March 5, dockworkers and apprentices accosted a sentry posted at the Customs House, and in the confusion, several soldiers fired into the crowd. Crispus Attucks, a dockworker and rope-maker of African and Wampanoag Indian descent, became one of the first casualties of the American Revolution when he and four others were killed.

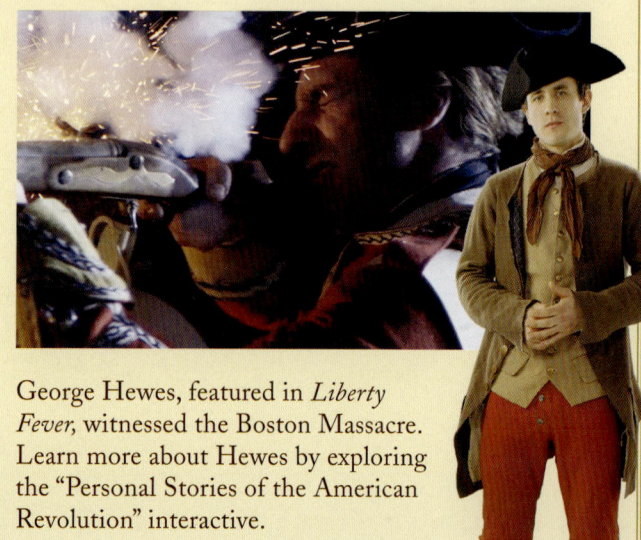

George Hewes, featured in *Liberty Fever*, witnessed the Boston Massacre. Learn more about Hewes by exploring the "Personal Stories of the American Revolution" interactive.

14 · *Jamestown-Yorktown Foundation*

★ **PORTABLE LAP DESK,** mid-1700s. This lap desk was once owned by Francis Marion of South Carolina, known as the "Swamp Fox." Lap desks were portable writing surfaces that could be used in the home or while traveling. Letters were a key means of communications between the colonies.

★ ★ ★

WATCH *CHANGING RELATIONSHIPS*. In the Red Lion Tavern theater, learn more about events that led to the American Revolution.

An Emerging American Identity

As opposition to British policies grew more widespread, the colonists recognized the need to work cooperatively together. Some colonies organized groups into "committees of correspondence" for more effective communication. The First Continental Congress met in Philadelphia in September 1774 and agreed to stop trade with England if Parliament did not repeal the Intolerable Acts.

The collective defiance of the First Continental Congress angered the British government, but most of the colonies' royal governors and other crown-appointed officials lacked the power to control or punish the Patriots. In colony after colony, Patriots set up their own committees or associations to enforce the policies of the Continental Congress. Among these were committees of safety, established for the defense of the colonies should the British government use military force.

"*The distinction between Virginians, Pennsylvanians, New Yorkers, and New Englanders are no more. I AM Not a Virginian, But an American…*"

– **PATRICK HENRY,** 1774

AMERICAN REVOLUTION GALLERIES

The War Begins

*F*ew British troops were stationed in the 13 Colonies, but there was a small group of British army soldiers in Boston, Massachusetts. In early 1775, King George III and Parliament declared Massachusetts to be in a state of rebellion. British officials in England began making plans to use these well-trained, professional soldiers to re-establish royal authority and control in the colony.

With Massachusetts in rebellion, the British military governor, Thomas Gage, ordered 800 British troops to march from Boston to Concord in April 1775 to seize military materiel stored there. Shots were exchanged with local militiamen as the British passed through Lexington. Often referred to as the "shot heard 'round the world," news of this exchange traveled quickly, and fighting continued in Concord as the British marched back to Boston.

The Second Continental Congress convened in May 1775, authorized a Continental Army, and appointed Virginian George Washington as its commander-in-chief. The war had begun and would continue for more than six years.

BROWN BESS MUSKET, *English, 1742.*

"The barbarous Murders on our innocent Brethren on Wednesday the 19th instant, has made it absolutely necessary that we immediately raise an Army to defend our Wives and Children."

— JOSEPH WARREN, APRIL 1775

The War Comes to Virginia

The earliest major battles of the Revolution were fought in New England, but the war spread quickly to other parts of North America. In Virginia, Royal Governor Lord Dunmore fled Williamsburg in June 1775, taking refuge aboard a British ship in the Chesapeake Bay. Seeking support of Loyalists, he attempted to organize a military campaign to retake Virginia. He also issued what is known now as Dunmore's Proclamation in November 1775, declaring Patriots to be traitors and offering freedom to any Patriot-owned slaves willing to fight for the British.

Dunmore established a fortified base at the port of Norfolk with a small force of British regulars, Loyalist militia and freed slaves. Virginia's Patriot government sent troops to dislodge the British from their position. The ensuing Battle of Great Bridge on the way to Norfolk was over in 30 minutes. A defeated Dunmore was forced to abandon Norfolk. The Virginians occupied the town, and Dunmore left the colony in August 1776.

African Americans fought on both sides at the Battle of Great Bridge. Liberated slaves formed a major part of Lord Dunmore's small army there and continued to fight in later battles. On the Patriot side, William (Billy) Flora, a free African American, was one of the heroes of the battle. Billy Flora is featured in the introductory film, *Liberty Fever*. Learn more about Billy Flora in the "Personal Stories of the American Revolution" interactive.

AMERICAN REVOLUTION GALLERIES

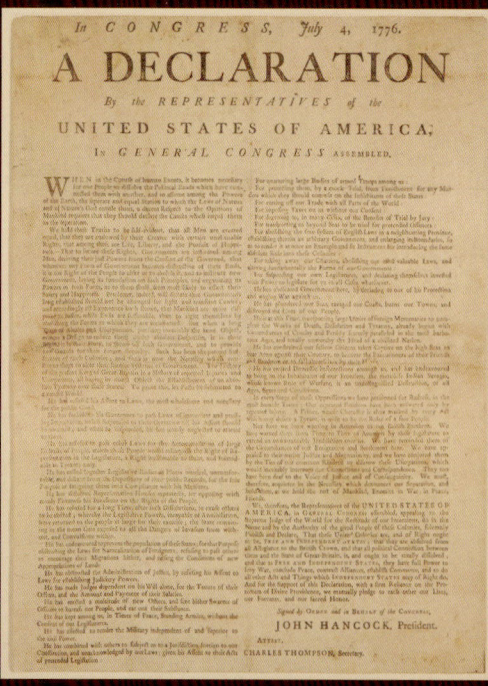

 DECLARATION OF INDEPENDENCE BROADSIDE — *This rare broadside printing of the Declaration of Independence was co-published in Boston, Massachusetts, on or about July 18, 1776, by John Gill and Edward E. Powers and Nathaniel Willis. This historic document predates the handwritten parchment copy signed by members of Congress in August 1776 and the official printing with the names of the signers authorized by Congress in January 1777.*

Independence!

*F*ew Americans were thinking about separation from the mother country in the spring of 1775, but as the year progressed, many began to change their minds. Thomas Paine's *Common Sense*, published in January 1776, reached out to ordinary people with plain language and an unprecedented common style that drew thousands into the political debate. A supporter of the American cause, he jolted reluctant colonists off the fence to fight for independence.

After Richard Henry Lee of Virginia introduced a motion for independence, Congress appointed a committee to prepare a formal statement explaining why the colonists were separating from Great Britain. Congress adopted the Declaration of Independence, largely the work of Thomas Jefferson, on July 4, 1776.

Spreading The Word

*I*n the 1700s, the only effective mass communication was the printed word. Once adopted, the Continental Congress ordered printed copies of the Declaration be sent to the provincial assemblies and committees of safety and to be read aloud to the public. When these copies reached their destinations, local printers re-printed the document in newspapers or as special single sheet "broadside" for further distribution. It was even published in German so immigrants who did not speak English well could read it. By August 2, it was published in South Carolina, and by the middle of August, it had been printed in Britain.

SABER, *made by silversmith Richard Humphreys of Philadelphia in 1776. During the Revolution, the eagle became one of the symbols of the new United States.*

Virginia Declaration of Rights

In June 1776, Virginia adopted George Mason's Declaration of Rights. Declaring, "All men are by nature equally free and independent, and have certain inherent rights," the ideas presented drew upon the foundations of British and Virginia law and government.

The first Philadelphia printing of the Virginia Declaration of Rights appeared in *The Pennsylvania Gazette* on June 12, 1776. The day before the Second Continental Congress had assigned a committee to write a statement making the case for independence. The Virginia Declaration of Rights undoubtedly influenced Thomas Jefferson and other committee members as they drafted the Declaration of Independence.

AMERICAN REVOLUTION GALLERIES

The New Nation Enters the World Stage

Desperately short of military supplies, the Continental Congress realized they needed foreign help if Americans were to secure their independence. France, England's traditional enemy, hoped to use the American rebellion to weaken British power. At first, the French were reluctant to openly support the American rebels, but they began secretly sending gunpowder, weapons and clothing, as well as extending credit to America. This policy of "watchful waiting" continued until the Americans formally declared their independence and demonstrated they were able to defend it.

In September 1776, the Continental Congress sent a delegation headed by Benjamin Franklin to Paris to seek an official alliance with France. At first, the French foreign minister delayed, but news of the stunning American victory at the Battle of Saratoga, New York, in October 1777 tipped the balance. The French publicly entered the war in 1778 by signing a "Treaty of Alliance" and a treaty of "Amity and Commerce" with the United States. These alliances transformed a colonial dispute with Great Britain into a world war.

The *Saratoga: First Great Victory* film features the Battle of Saratoga and its importance as a turning point in the Revolutionary War.

LOUIS XVI, KING OF FRANCE, *from the studio of Joseph Boze, circa 1784. King Louis XVI secretly sent supplies, ammunition and guns to the Patriots and in 1778 signed a formal alliance with America. Ironically, he and his queen, Marie Antoinette, were executed in 1793 during the French Revolution, an action inspired by the American Revolution.*

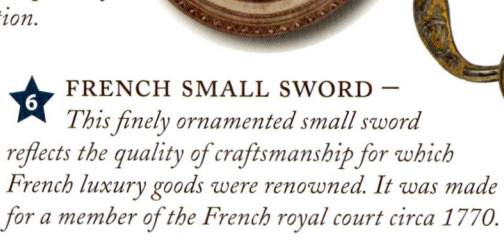

6 FRENCH SMALL SWORD — *This finely ornamented small sword reflects the quality of craftsmanship for which French luxury goods were renowned. It was made for a member of the French royal court circa 1770.*

American Loyalists

While some British Loyalists fled to Great Britain, most remained in America. Loyalists came from all social and economic groups and included small farmers, artisans, shopkeepers, wealthy merchants, British officials, Anglican clergymen and recent immigrants. The greatest number came from the middle colonies, especially New York and New Jersey, but a significant number lived in Georgia and the backcountry of the Carolinas.

Loyalists believed resistance to legitimate British government was wrong. They tended to be cautious and often feared the disorder and violence of mob rule that threatened their status and property. About 15 to 20 percent of the colonies' white population could be described as Loyalists, although an equal number tried to avoid getting involved on either side.

Outspoken supporters of the king were often harassed and subjected to humiliation, and many learned to keep their political beliefs quiet to avoid having their property confiscated by the Patriots. Others took an active part in the fighting.

Scene from *Changing Relationships* film.

BRITISH OFFICER'S PISTOLS, *pair of silver-mounted flintlock pistols, made by Joseph Griffin of Birmingham, England, circa 1767-68.*

AMERICAN REVOLUTION GALLERIES

Women and the American Revolution

Before the war began, women supported the Patriot cause by refusing to drink tea or buy imported British goods. During the war, American wives, mothers and daughters also made important contributions to winning independence, especially by spinning and weaving cloth. Women also filled economic roles usually reserved for men such as managing farms, running businesses and working in non-traditional occupations. More than half the workers in the Continental Army's wartime ammunition factory in Philadelphia were women.

Many poorer women followed their soldier husbands in the army, supporting themselves by mending uniforms, doing laundry and nursing the sick and wounded. While George Washington was concerned about the number of women who followed the army, he also recognized their value.

EXPLORE PERSONAL STORIES of ordinary people who played a role in the Revolution.

The conflict between the 13 Colonies and Britain at times led to family disputes. In South Carolina, Isabella Ferguson had a bitter quarrel with her brother-in-law Colonel James Ferguson, a Loyalist. When James tried to recruit her husband, Isabella responded, "I am a rebel, my brothers are rebels, and the dog Trip is a rebel, too." She then threatened to leave her husband if he chose to fight for the British. He did not. Listen to the stories of Isabella and Trip on the "Personal Stories of the Revolution" interactive.

22 ✦ *Jamestown-Yorktown Foundation*

African-American Life and the Revolution

Many African Americans, free and enslaved, fought in the war. African-American minutemen were present at Lexington, and others fought valiantly at the Battles of Bunker and Breed's Hill. As the war progressed, local and national policies excluded African Americans as soldiers, but by 1777 shortages of Continental Army troops soon led to the recruitment of free and enslaved African Americans.

Free blacks enlisted willingly, lured by the promise of money and land. While policies for enlistment of enslaved men varied from place to place, many were offered freedom in exchange for service. Enslaved African Americans could also serve as substitutes for their owners. Within the Continental Army, African Americans fought side-by-side with white soldiers, but several states, such as Rhode Island, also formed mostly black units. While many African Americans were armed, most performed support services such as wagoners, pilots, blacksmiths, carpenters, cooks, laborers, servants and even spies. A few African American women acted as nurses or cooks.

After Lord Dunmore's defeat at the Battle of Great Bridge, runaways continued to seek refuge with the British, serving in non-combatant roles similar to those in the Continental Army.

SUBSTITUTE ENLISTMENT CERTIFICATION FOR SLAVE JACK,

Woburn, Massachusetts, November 17, 1777. John Austin, Jr., of Charlestown, Massachusetts, avoided serving in the Continental Army by sending his enslaved man, Jack, in his place. Jack may have gotten his freedom in return for his service.

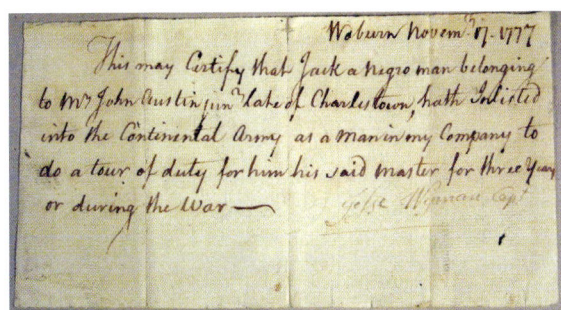

What was it like to go undercover and spy on the British during the American Revolution? James Lafayette did it against all odds. An enslaved African American in New Kent County when the British invaded Virginia in 1781, James soon found himself working for the Continental Army under the Marquis de Lafayette. Serving as a spy, he infiltrated British camps, supplying important information to the Americans that would influence the outcome of the war. In 1786, the Virginia General Assembly granted James his freedom for his service. Hear James tell his story on the "Personal Stories of the Revolution" interactive.

AMERICAN REVOLUTION GALLERIES

> "When your army entered the country of the Seneca Nation we called you Town Destroyer; and to this day when that name is heard our women look behind them and turn pale."
>
> — CORNPLANTER, Seneca War Chief, to George Washington, 1790

The Indians at War

For Indians of Eastern North America, the American Revolution was one more challenge in their continuing fight to preserve their lands and way of life. At first neither the British nor the Patriots were particularly interested in gaining their support, but both sides soon changed their minds.

In the North, four of the six Iroquois nations chose to ally with the British, and the Iroquois played a prominent role in the Saratoga campaign. In the South, the Cherokee joined with British Loyalists in attacks on American frontier posts, and the Creek and Choctaw fought alongside British troops in the defense of the British colony of Florida.

Some other Indian groups, usually those living in areas already settled by colonists, decided supporting the Patriots was the wisest choice. The Stockbridge Indians of Massachusetts and the Catawba Indians of the Carolinas are just two of several Indian communities who fought hard for American independence.

Regardless of side, the war would have damaging consequences for most Indian tribes.

> "I fought against the British for your sake, The British have Disappeared, and you are free. Yet from me the British took nothing, nor have I gained anything from their defeat. I pursued the deer for my subsistence, the deer are disappearing, and I must starve. God ordained me for the forest, and my ambition is the shade, but the strength in my arms decays, and my feet fail in the chase, the hand which fought for your liberties is now open for your relief. In my Youth I bled in battle, that you might be independent. Let not my heart in my old age bleed for the want of your commission."
>
> — PETER HARRIS, 1818

Peter Harris, a Catawba Indian, petitioned South Carolina for a pension. In response, he received $60 a year for his Revolutionary War services. Hear Peter's story on the "Personal Stories of the Revolution" interactive.

Jamestown-Yorktown Foundation

The War Moves South

By 1778, the British were concerned that, although their army could take and hold cities such as New York and Philadelphia, it had not succeeded in destroying the Continental Army. When France entered the conflict, the British needed a new strategy and shifted the main theater of the war to the South.

This approach met with early success when the British easily took Savannah, Georgia, in late 1778. In 1780, the British forced the Americans to surrender Charleston, South Carolina, and nearly 5,500 Continental Army soldiers were captured. After this disastrous American defeat, General Charles Cornwallis worked to organize southern Loyalists and secure the Carolinas for the king.

In the summer of 1780, General Horatio Gates took command of the Patriot forces in the South, but in August, Cornwallis decisively defeated him at Camden, South Carolina, and the Patriot cause seemed hopeless. Washington then sent General Nathanael Greene to take charge of what remained of the American army in the South. Instead of confronting the British directly, Greene harassed the enemy, drawing Cornwallis further into the backcountry and away from resupply.

Two subsequent, critical American victories at King's Mountain and Cowpens, South Carolina, led General Greene to directly confront Cornwallis at Guilford Courthouse, North Carolina, in March 1781. Although the battle was technically a British victory, Cornwallis suffered more than 500 casualties. Severely weakened, he abandoned his attempt to subdue North Carolina and moved north to join up with other British forces in Virginia.

★★★

Search and investigate important battles of the Revolutionary War on the "Battle of the Revolutionary War" interactive.

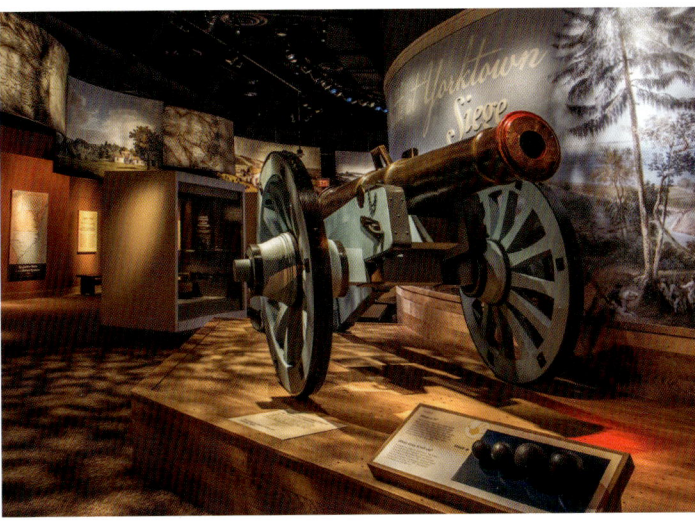

The War in the South gallery

GENERAL DANIEL MORGAN *miniature portrait, James Peale, circa 1790. Morgan commanded a light infantry corps in the South under Nathanael Greene. Morgan's force virtually destroyed Banastre Tarleton's British Legion at the Battle of Cowpens.*

American Revolution Museum at Yorktown ✚ 25

AMERICAN REVOLUTION GALLERIES

Siege of Yorktown – Surrender

In April 1781, British General Cornwallis abandoned North Carolina and marched to Virginia. After an unsuccessful pursuit of a small Patriot force led by the Marquis de Lafayette, Cornwallis decided to move nearer the coast and establish a fortified base at Yorktown near the Chesapeake Bay. Meanwhile in New York, four regiments of French soldiers under the Comte de Rochambeau had joined with Washington's Continental Army.

In August, Rochambeau learned a powerful French fleet, under Admiral de Grasse, was planning to sail to the Chesapeake Bay and be available for joint operations. In New York General Washington and Rochambeau plotted to trap Cornwallis at Yorktown and began the 400-mile journey south. In early September, the French fleet met and drove off a British naval force at the Battle of the Capes. By October, Cornwallis was under siege, surrounded, outnumbered and cut off from reinforcements. For two weeks, heavy artillery fire battered British defensive works. With no sign of relief, Cornwallis surrendered his entire army of 8,000 men on October 19, 1781.

CHARLES, 1ST MARQUIS CORNWALLIS *portrait by Daniel Gardner, London.*

British General Cornwallis commanded the British troops during the Siege of Yorktown.

THE SIEGE OF YORKTOWN *unfolds in a 180-degree surround screen theater, complete with rumbling seats, wind, smoke and the smell of battle.*

Yorktown's Sunken Fleet

By the end of the siege, most of Cornwallis' warships, as well as merchant and transport vessels, lay at the bottom of the York River. Some were scuttled by the British to create a defensive barrier offshore, some were sacrificed to prevent capture and others were sunk by French artillery fire. Between 1975 and 1981, a scientific underwater survey located the remains of nine British ships. Underwater archaeologists excavated one of these ships, the *Betsy,* a two-masted brig built in England that probably carried supplies to the British forces in America. View recovered items from the *Betsy,* including lumber, tools, a bucket, a whistle and even rat skulls.

★ ★ ★

WHAT'S A SIEGE?
A siege is a military blockade where an army surrounds a city, cuts off its supplies and communication, and usually assaults its defenses.

Artifacts recovered from the BETSY, *on loan from the Virginia Department of Historic Resources.*

AMERICAN REVOLUTION GALLERIES

The Treaty of Paris

News of the British defeat at Yorktown was the final straw for the British people, and Parliament decided to end this expensive, unwinnable war. Although peace was not finally concluded for nearly two more years, further military action was limited to a few minor skirmishes.

The final treaty, signed in Paris in 1783, recognized an independent United States with boundaries extending from Canada and the Great Lakes southward to Florida and west to the Mississippi River. Indian rights to such lands were ignored by both the British and American treaty negotiators.

The Confederation Congress was the new government of the United States. Formally established in March 1781, it replaced the Second Continental Congress and governed under the Articles of Confederation.

SILVER MEDAL *commemorating the recognition of the United States in 1782 by Frisia, one of seven provinces of the Dutch Republic. Frisia's action led to the recognition of the American nation by the Dutch Republic. An American Indian princess represents America with a set of broken shackles beneath, while the goddess Britannia stands above a snake in the grass.*

"*Our Country, My Friend, is not yet out of Danger. There are great Difficulties in our Constitution and Situation.*"

— JOHN ADAMS to Samuel Adams, 1784

The Enduring Problem of Slavery

The American Revolution dramatically shifted public opinion on the issue of slavery. By 1784, five northern states had passed laws that would end slavery either immediately or at some fixed future date. Even in the South, many prominent individuals freed their slaves. The reason given most often was that slavery was "inconsistent with the principles of the new republic."

American activists worked with their English counterparts first to abolish the slave trade and then to abolish slavery. To do this they used methods familiar to us today, including slogans, merchandising and product placement.

Nevertheless, no state south of Pennsylvania ended slavery. In fact, during the post-war period, slavery and the plantation economy expanded in the South, spreading westward into new lands. Many Southerners believed emancipation would cause economic collapse, and they worried about the political and social consequences of creating hundreds of thousands of new African-American citizens. Fear of retaliation by former slaves upon slaveholders led Thomas Jefferson and others to propose emancipation plans for the South requiring re-settlement of freed slaves outside the United States, but such plans were impractical and never developed wide support.

8 JASPERWARE ANTI-SLAVERY MEDALLION, *British, circa 1786. Josiah Wedgwood & William Hackwood Inscribed, "Am I not a man and a brother?"*

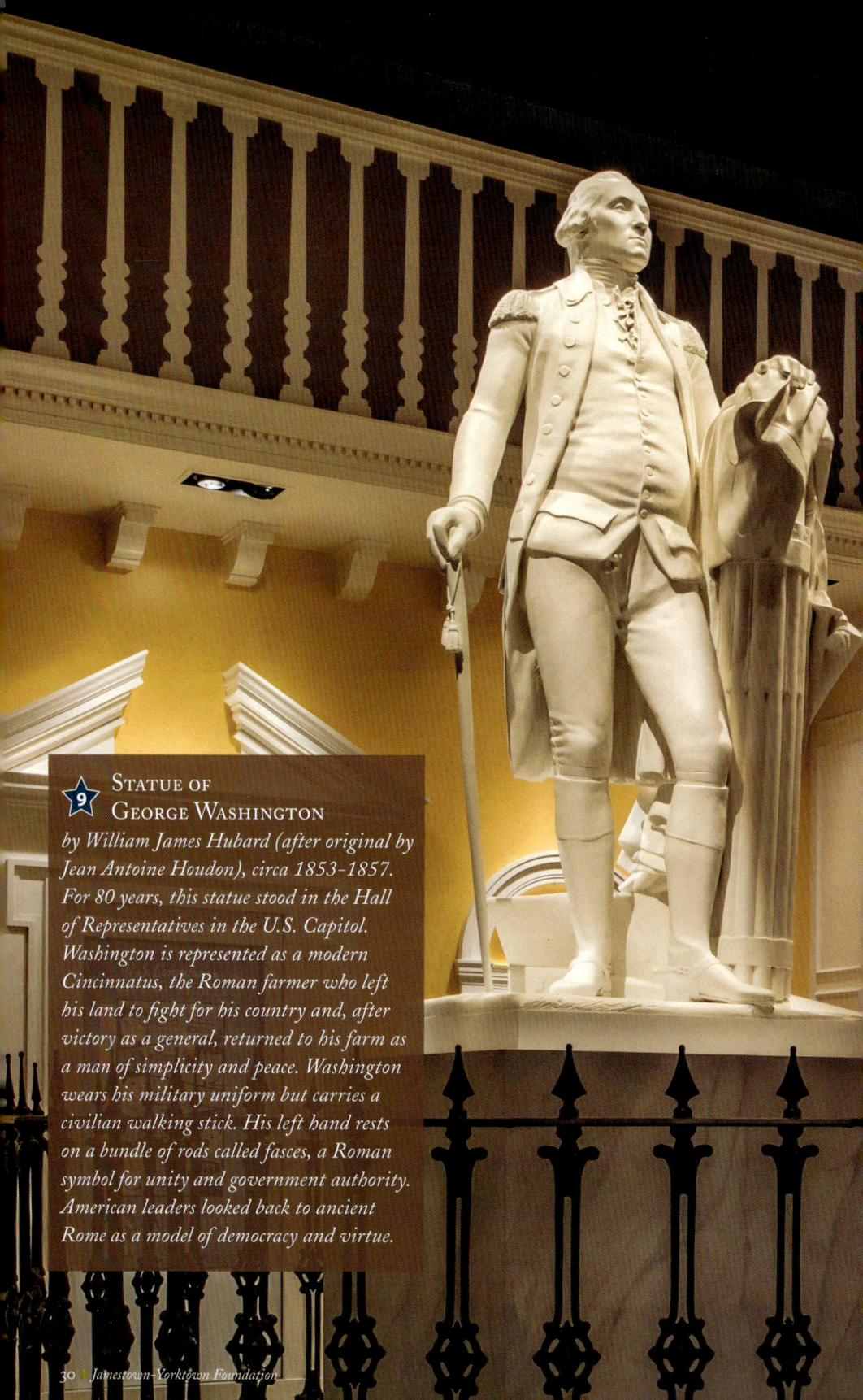

⭐9 STATUE OF GEORGE WASHINGTON

by William James Hubard (after original by Jean Antoine Houdon), circa 1853–1857. For 80 years, this statue stood in the Hall of Representatives in the U.S. Capitol. Washington is represented as a modern Cincinnatus, the Roman farmer who left his land to fight for his country and, after victory as a general, returned to his farm as a man of simplicity and peace. Washington wears his military uniform but carries a civilian walking stick. His left hand rests on a bundle of rods called fasces, a Roman symbol for unity and government authority. American leaders looked back to ancient Rome as a model of democracy and virtue.

AMERICAN REVOLUTION GALLERIES

Governing a New Nation

*I*n 1787, the Federal Constitutional Convention convened in Philadelphia, Pennsylvania, to discuss revising the Articles of Confederation. Because the individual states were wary of giving the national government too much power, the Confederation Congress did not have the authority to levy taxes, draft troops, or regulate trade and commerce.

Instead of revising the existing Articles of Confederation, many of the convention's delegates proposed a strong, central, federal government featuring the separation of powers and a system of checks and balances.

From the beginning, the new system faced opposition from Anti-Federalists, those who saw it as a threat to their liberties. After its supporters, the Federalists, promised to add amendments protecting individual rights, the states ratified the plan. By April 1789, the new United States Constitution and Bill of Rights were in effect, and George Washington had been elected the first president.

View our film, *Creation of the Constitution*, to learn about the compromises required to establish a new government for a new nation.

EPAULETTE STAR, *belonging to George Washington, Philadelphia, 1799. This epaulette was made for Washington after he left the presidency and was re-appointed as commanding general of the new United States Army. An epaulette is an ornamental decoration worn on the shoulder as a symbol of rank.*

GEORGE WASHINGTON INAUGURAL BUTTON, *American, circa 1789. People attending George Washington's inauguration in New York City could purchase souvenirs such a this button to commemorate the occasion.*

American Revolution Museum at Yorktown ✦ 31

AMERICAN REVOLUTION GALLERIES

America Open to People of Many Lands

In 1789, the United States embarked on a bold new experiment. People who had shared a "common cause," the struggle for independence, no longer thought of themselves as residents of individual states, but now began thinking of themselves as Americans. The new Federal Constitution and Bill of Rights provided a framework that protected individual rights and balanced freedom with order, and rights with responsibilities.

This new country enticed a fresh wave of immigrants from Europe and the Caribbean who looked to the United States as a land of opportunity. They hoped to improve themselves economically and escape Europe's wars and persecutions. Americans welcomed this new labor pool, and land speculators hoped to sell them land in the west.

Seeking cheap new lands, people traveled on rough trails and journeyed hundreds of miles on rivers, through forests and across mountains. Soon these settlers complained about the inconvenience and injustice of answering to a distant authority to the east. To promote an orderly expansion of settlement and strengthen the Union, the federal government encouraged the creation of new states.

10 FERRY MARKER *from South Brownsville, Pennsylvania, 1813. Features the dominant image of an American eagle with the inscription, "Liberty."*

✦ ✦ ✦
"The United States of America in 1791"
interactive map

The first United States census, taken in 1791 and mandated by the Constitution to apportion political representation and taxation, depicts an America significantly different from that of the colonial period. The nation had grown larger in population and territory. Many Americans had moved westward, settling new lands that had not been open to them during the colonial era. Internal migration also had become important, with people moving from one part of the country to another more frequently than in the past. Explore 1791 regions, boundaries, Indian lands, population, slavery and commerce on the interactive map.

LEGACY OF THE AMERICAN REVOLUTION

America – Yesterday and Today

Shared experiences of the Revolution helped shape a new distinctly American society. A rising middle class of small landowners, shopkeepers and urban artisans put the ideals of the Revolution into action by challenging the established order. The new government balanced freedom and individual rights with order and responsibility. Because sovereignty resided in the people, government was their servant, not their master. Most importantly, there was an emerging doctrine and an understanding of equality.

Through the years, these American ideals have inspired gradual, but continual, reforms, extending political rights and economic opportunities to a growing and diverse American population. Through times of struggle and national pride, the documents of the Revolution—the Declaration of Independence, United States Constitution and the Bill of Rights—have guided Americans and other nations around the world.

> ★ ★ ★
>
> By the end of the 1900s, more than 160 nations had adopted written charters largely based on the U.S. Constitution. Among these are the post-Soviet European countries of Hungary, Poland and Romania.

In 1765, colonists in Boston staged their first act of resistance to British policies at an elm tree near Boston Common. The tree became a symbol of defiance and came to be known as the Liberty Tree. Leave a message on our Liberty Tree, telling us what liberty means to you.

"The cause of America is in great measure the cause of all mankind."

– THOMAS PAINE, 1776

CONTINENTAL ARMY ENCAMPMENT

Explore the soldiers' tents, try on a regimental uniform, join in a wooden-musket drill and take in a flintlock musket or cannon demonstration. Speak with the surgeon to learn about period medical and surgical practices, try your hand at espionage or serve as the quartermaster to manage the troops.

The Continental Army encampment represents a section of an American regiment during the Revolutionary War. Laid out according to regulations written by Baron Friedrich von Steuben, Inspector General of the Continental Army, the camp includes soldier and officer tents, surgeon and quartermaster quarters, an earthen kitchen and a makeshift shelter used by families who followed the army.

Ordinary men from different social ranks, occupations and ethnic backgrounds joined the Continental Army out of patriotism, for adventure and for promises of money or land. More than 200,000 Americans fought in the army during the war, although many for

"I was now what I long wished to be, a soldier. I had obtained my heart's desire; it was now my business to prove myself equal to my profession."

— JOSEPH PLUMB MARTIN,
1830 memoir of a Revolutionary War soldier

short periods. Most were younger than 23 years old and owned little property. By comparison, the typical British soldier was an older-career soldier with greater training and experience.

At the beginning of the war, many units did not allow African Americans to serve. By the end of the long war, both free and enslaved African Americans had enlisted to fight for the Patriot cause. Enslaved men sometimes fought for the promise of freedom. Some were able to secure their freedom, but others ended up returned to a life of slavery.

Military training was necessary to transform civilian recruits into skilled, disciplined soldiers. In 1778, General George Washington appointed Baron von Steuben to be Inspector General of the Continental Army. His greatest contribution was to create a standard drill manual that improved the army's professionalism. Von Steuben taught the men military drills, tactics and weaponry. Sounds of drums and fifes conveyed orders in battle and regulated daily camp life. Military organization was critical to both the battlefield and life in camp. When organization broke down, the men suffered.

> ★ ★ ★
> Note that the higher the rank of the soldier, the higher the sides of the tent he lived in.

George Washington served as commander-in chief throughout the war without pay, and his men held him in high regard. He had to marshal his limited forces and supplies carefully and lead his men to critical victories, including Yorktown. Washington successfully used espionage, including secret codes and invisible inks, to get needed information upon which to base his decisions.

Both the Americans and the British had problems supplying their armies. Food, clothing, arms and other supplies were often inadequate and late arriving. Firsthand accounts indicate soldiers often received much less food than promised. Throughout the war, the American army suffered from a lack of clothing and tents due to shortages of cloth previously imported from England.

Poor diet and unsanitary camp conditions caused much sickness throughout the long war. Far more deaths in the army resulted from sickness and disease than from wounds received in battle. In 1777, General Washington ordered the entire army inoculated against smallpox. This bold, controversial move prevented widespread epidemics and probably helped America win the war.

Wives, daughters or mothers of soldiers unable to support themselves sometimes became "camp followers" who performed domestic chores, such as cooking, sewing, mending, laundry and nursing the sick and wounded. Doing this work freed the men for their military duties.

Commanders came to realize driving out these women could lead to the loss of good men. In return for their labors, women traveling with the army sought food, shelter and safety. Over the course of the American Revolution, thousands of women, along with many children, trailed behind the troops. These women needed the army, and the army needed them.

The reality confronted by all who chose to be with the Continental Army was a life of adversity, but their sacrifices ultimately led to American independence.

★ ★ ★

Popular culture often depicts Continental Army soldiers fighting from behind fences and trees, and this did happen occasionally in rough terrain. But American soldiers were trained and usually fought in the same kind of linear tactics used by European armies of the period. Men stood shoulder to shoulder, firing muskets or charging with bayonets, and advanced across the field of battle.

REVOLUTION-ERA FARM

Explore the annual cycle of work on a Tidewater Virginia farm. Plant, water or weed vegetables and herbs, comb cotton, "break" flax into fiber, preserve foodstuffs, make the bed, gather firewood, assist in preparing a meal or learn how farm families used herbs in cooking and medicines. When your work is done, play a game with your family.

The Revolution-era farm includes a typical 1770s house of the "middling sort," separate kitchen, quarter for enslaved African Americans, a tobacco barn, shed and gardens. During the American Revolution, the majority of Virginians were farmers who occupied humble rural dwellings. Edward Moss was a York County, Virginia, farmer during the Revolution. After his death, a probate inventory listing his possessions was made and dated May 15, 1786. His inventory was an important source of information for the re-creation of this farm.

Much of life on a typical farm, like that of Edward Moss, took place in and around the farmhouse. The house was not only for sleeping and storage, but also for eating, educating the children, enjoying pastimes and keeping accounts. Many other activities occurred outside the house in the nearby yard and outbuildings, including the kitchen.

Tobacco, corn and flax exemplify crops grown by Virginia farmers in the late 1700s. Prior to the Revolution, tobacco was the primary crop, grown for export to England. The farmer hung tobacco leaves from poles in the barn to cure it as part of a yearlong process required to make a profit from this cash crop. With the interruption of trade during the war, farmers grew corn for food, cash and animal fodder. Growing flax and cotton for cloth production also became a necessity and patriotic duty. Throughout the year, families planted and harvested a variety of vegetables and herbs.

Common breeds of fowl—such as ducks, chickens and turkeys—roamed freely throughout the farm. Important as a source of food, these birds also helped control insect pests. Farms of the time also had larger animals such as sheep, cattle and pigs.

In the detached log kitchen, products of the farm were cooked, and foodstuffs were preserved by drying, pickling and salting. One corner of the room held the bedroll for an enslaved person living and working in the kitchen.

Slavery was prevalent throughout colonial America and an inescapable aspect of daily life in Virginia. A middling Virginia farmer would likely have owned six or fewer slaves, including children, and occasionally hired slaves from other farms. Enslaved people living on this farm probably slept in the kitchen or barn or in the separate quarters provided for them. While their housing was meager, enslaved people did have some personal belongings and kept their own small gardens.

The Revolutionary War presented some enslaved Virginians the possibility of freedom by serving in the military. Virginia's Lord Dunmore offered freedom to those enslaved by Patriot rebels if they joined his British army. Some ran away to fight. Others chose to remain in slavery, perhaps fearful of being caught and punished or concerned about leaving family behind.

Women and children, both free and enslaved, found their wartime workload greatly increased from making items previously purchased, such as cloth, candles and soap. If the men of the family left for army or militia service, the strain on the family became even greater. If an army marched past or occupied the farm, the soldiers demanded food, firewood and more. After the war,

"…the (Virginia) houses here are almost all of wood, covered with the same; the roof with shingles, the sides and ends with thin boards, and not always lathed and plastered within; only those of the better sort are finished in that manner…The windows of the better sort have glass in them; the rest have none, and only wooden shutters…."

— J. F. D. SMYTH, ESQUIRE,
1784 memoir of travels through 1770s America

many farmers submitted claims for items taken by both the British and American armies. Everyone living through the American Revolution had to adapt to the changes happening around them. Their choices, and the consequences of their decisions, would shape the future of the new nation.

★ ★ ★

Edward Moss lived on a farm in York County with his wife, Martha, and four children. When he died in 1786, he owned six enslaved men, women and children. This re-created farm is based on his inventory, as well as extensive historical research into Virginia houses and outbuildings of 18th-century Virginia. Compare the house, kitchen and slave quarter to see different building methods of the time.

American Revolution Museum at Yorktown ✦ 39

AMERICAN REVOLUTION TIMELINE

October 1760: George III becomes King of England and ruler of the British Empire. He pursues stricter policies toward the colonies.

February 1763: The Treaty of Paris ends the Seven Years' War. France, decisively defeated, is forced to give up most of its claims to North American territory.

March 1765: Parliament passes the Stamp Act, imposing new taxes on Americans. Angry mobs throughout the colonies reject the tax and threaten stamp distributors.

June 1767: Parliament enacts the Townshend Acts, imposing duties on glass, tea and other items. Americans react by refusing to buy British goods.

April 1770: Realizing the Townshend Acts are discouraging the purchasing of British goods, Parliament repeals all taxes except those on tea.

Changing Relationships film.

December 1773: Patriots dressed as Indians board ships in Boston harbor and dump more than 300 chests of tea overboard to protest the tea tax.

March 1774: Parliament passes the Boston Port Act, closing the harbor to all seaborne trade as punishment for the Boston Tea Party.

September 1774: Representatives from the colonies meet together as the First Continental Congress to forge a unified response to British policies.

October 1774: Colonel Andrew Lewis of Virginia defeats the Shawnee Indians under Chief Cornstalk in the Battle of Point Pleasant, securing Virginia's western frontier.

Changing Relationships film.

April 1775: British troops exchange gunfire with Massachusetts minutemen at Lexington and Concord. The British army in Boston is besieged by American militiamen.

June 1775: At the Battle of Bunker Hill, near Boston, British troops defeat the Americans, but suffer heavy losses. George Washington is appointed commander-in-chief of the Patriot army.

November 1775: Lord Dunmore, Virginia's royal governor, issues a proclamation offering freedom to all slaves owned by Patriots who are willing to fight with the British.

December 1775: British soldiers under Royal Governor Dunmore's command are defeated by Virginia troops at the Battle of Great Bridge, Virginia.

January 1776: Thomas Paine's pamphlet *Common Sense* is published. It wins thousands of American colonists over to the idea of American independence.

May 1776: France begins secretly sending money and military supplies to the American rebels.

June 1776: The Virginia Revolutionary Convention enacts George Mason's Declaration of Rights, the first bill of rights to be adopted in America.

July 1776: The Continental Congress resolves that the colonies ought to be "free and independent States." Congress approves the Declaration of Independence.

December 1776: Crossing the Delaware River on Christmas night, Washington wins a stunning victory at Trenton, New Jersey, and gives new hope to the Patriot cause.

September 1777: At the Battle of Brandywine, Pennsylvania, Washington is unable to stop the British as they advance and occupy Philadelphia.

October 1777: Instead of retreating, Washington takes the offensive and launches a bold, but unsuccessful, attack on the British at Germantown before going into winter quarters.

October 1777: British General John Burgoyne is forced to surrender his entire army of about 6,000 men at Saratoga, New York.

Winter 1777-1778: Washington's army moves into winter quarters at Valley Forge, Pennsylvania. Severe weather and shortages of food cause terrible hardships for the soldiers.

Liberty Fever film.

February 1778: France openly enters the war against Great Britain by signing a Treaty of Alliance and Commerce with the United States.

June 1778: Washington attacks the British under General Henry Clinton at Monmouth Court House, New Jersey. The battle ends in a draw.

December 1778: The British change their strategy and begin to focus on the southern states, first by capturing Savannah, Georgia.

Fall 1779: An American expedition under General John Sullivan devastates the homeland of Britain's Iroquois allies in western New York.

May 1780: Charleston, South Carolina, falls to the British, and 5,500 American troops are captured in the worst American defeat of the Revolutionary War.

August 1780: An American army under General Gates suffers a humiliating defeat at the hands of British General Cornwallis at Camden, South Carolina.

October 1780: At the Battle of King's Mountain, South Carolina, a group of frontier Patriot militiamen kill or capture more than 1,000 Loyalist fighters.

Changing Relationships film.

AMERICAN REVOLUTION TIMELINE

January 1781: In a brilliant victory at Cowpens, South Carolina, American General Daniel Morgan practically destroys a British force led by Colonel Banastre Tarleton.

March 1781: At the battle of Guilford Court House, North Carolina, British General Cornwallis claims victory, but suffers heavy losses. He moves his army north to Virginia and ultimately establishes a base at Yorktown.

August 1781: Washington and French General Rochambeau decide to march from New York to Virginia and trap Cornwallis.

September 5, 1781: In a major sea battle, known as the Battle of the Capes, French Admiral de Grasse's fleet drives off a British naval force attempting to assist Cornwallis.

October 6, 1781: The allied army, numbering more than 15,000 men, surrounds Yorktown and besieges British forces encamped there.

October 19, 1781: Cornwallis surrenders his army of about 7,000 British and German soldiers to the allied American-French force of Washington and Rochambeau.

March 1782: After learning of the surrender of Cornwallis at Yorktown, Lord North resigns as prime minister of Great Britain. Peace negotiations with the United States begin.

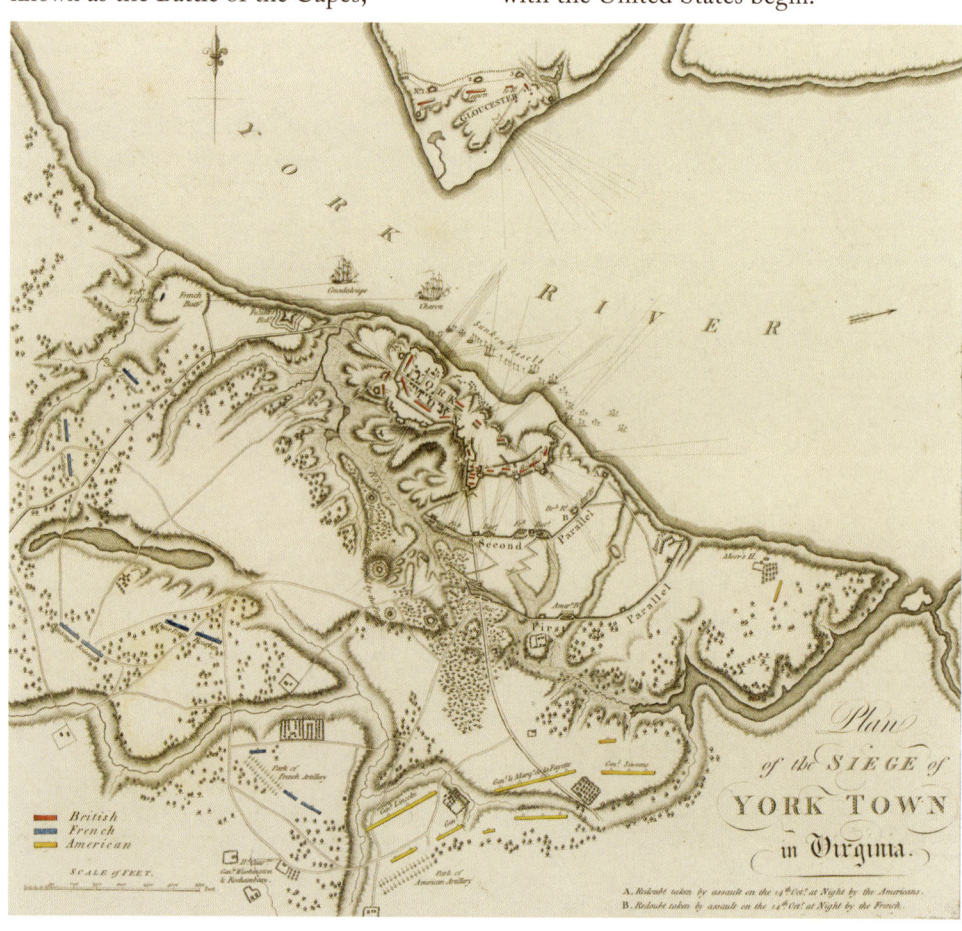

Plan of the Siege of York Town in Virginia, London, 1787.

Re-created Continental Army encampment.

August 1782: The last fighting of the war between American and British soldiers occurs in South Carolina.

December 1782: British forces evacuate Charleston, South Carolina.

July 1783: The Supreme Court of Massachusetts declares slavery illegal in that state.

September 1783: The final treaties ending hostilities are signed in Paris. The last British troops in the United States leave New York in November.

January 1786: Virginia adopts Thomas Jefferson's Statute for Religious Freedom, which later serves as a model for the First Amendment to the U.S. Constitution.

Summer 1786: America suffers from a post-war economic depression. The weak Confederation government is unable to solve the nation's problems.

September 1786: Representatives from five of the states meet to discuss interstate commerce. They propose a new convention to meet in 1787 to revise the Articles of Confederation.

Winter 1786-1787: American forces suppress "Shay's Rebellion," an uprising by New England farmers who fear their land will be seized for back taxes and debts.

May 1787: Delegates meet in Philadelphia to discuss revising the Articles of Confederation. The delegates decide instead to create an entirely new, federal form of government.

September 1787: The delegates at the Philadelphia convention agree on a final draft of the proposed new federal constitution and send it to the states for approval.

June 1788: New Hampshire becomes the ninth state to ratify the Constitution, putting it into effect. Within a month, Virginia and New York follow suit.

April 1789: The First Federal Congress convenes in New York City. George Washington is inaugurated as the first president of the United States under the new Constitution.

September 1789: Congress sends 12 constitutional amendments protecting individual rights to the states for approval.

March 1791: Vermont becomes the first new state to enter the Union after the original thirteen colonies.

December 1791: Virginia becomes the eleventh state to ratify the first 10 amendments, known as the Bill of Rights, to the Constitution.

SHACKLES, *West African, circa 1800. This type of shackle was used on transatlantic slave ships. By 1784, five northern states had passed laws that would end slavery, but during the post-war period, slavery expanded in the South and spread into new western lands.*

Colonial Crossword

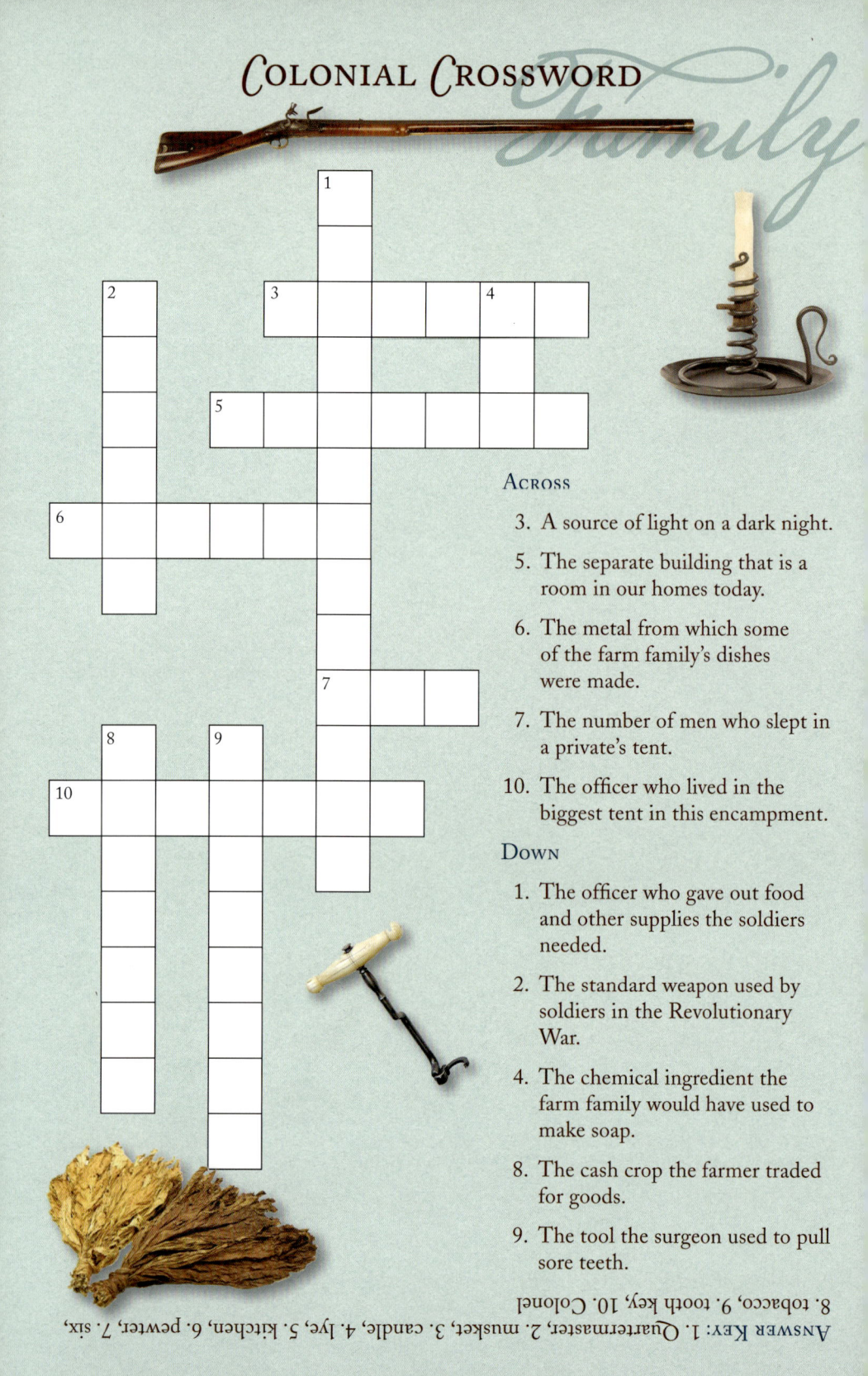

Across

3. A source of light on a dark night.
5. The separate building that is a room in our homes today.
6. The metal from which some of the farm family's dishes were made.
7. The number of men who slept in a private's tent.
10. The officer who lived in the biggest tent in this encampment.

Down

1. The officer who gave out food and other supplies the soldiers needed.
2. The standard weapon used by soldiers in the Revolutionary War.
4. The chemical ingredient the farm family would have used to make soap.
8. The cash crop the farmer traded for goods.
9. The tool the surgeon used to pull sore teeth.

Answer Key: 1. Quartermaster, 2. musket, 3. candle, 4. lye, 5. kitchen, 6. pewter, 7. six, 8. tobacco, 9. tooth key, 10. Colonel

Jamestown-Yorktown Foundation

Continental Army Camp Word Search

Fun

E	L	F	I	R	C	A	N	N	O	N	S	I	N	V
L	A	C	A	M	P	K	I	T	C	H	E	N	A	X
O	A	E	Z	B	B	N	A	A	G	F	B	V	B	C
R	E	I	D	L	O	S	H	M	Q	B	Z	R	P	O
C	N	R	O	C	I	R	T	E	K	N	A	L	B	R
S	O	W	L	U	B	A	Y	O	N	E	T	T	A	N
L	E	A	V	Y	Q	N	D	B	N	F	J	Y	N	W
I	G	S	E	I	L	P	P	U	S	E	R	P	V	A
V	R	H	O	Q	K	Z	N	R	E	T	N	A	L	L
Y	U	I	H	A	R	D	B	R	E	A	D	Z	S	L
H	S	N	Z	I	T	I	K	Z	H	C	O	A	P	I
U	G	G	J	H	M	M	K	M	D	C	I	G	X	S
R	U	T	Y	Y	Y	P	J	S	B	M	W	F	D	P
W	Z	O	K	X	F	D	T	N	E	T	W	D	F	R
Z	E	N	Y	D	F	J	L	A	R	E	N	E	G	O

SOLDIER   WASHINGTON   CAMP KITCHEN
CANNON   CORNWALLIS   HARDBREAD
TENT   BLANKET   RIFLE
OFFICER   LANTERN   BAYONET
SURGEON   GENERAL   TRICORN

★ ★ ★ **DIRECTIONS** ★ ★ ★

Find and circle the words in the list. You will find words running up, down, across, diagonal, forwards and backwards. Good luck!

American Revolution Museum at Yorktown ✦ 45

Crack The Code

General George Washington used spies and secret codes to get and share information during the American Revolution. Can you crack the code to find the secret message below?

★ ★ ★ DIRECTIONS ★ ★ ★

Use the numbers below to identify each letter in the message. The first number tells you the line in the song; the second number tells you the word in that line; the third number tells you the letter.

Example   121
                   446   The word is DOG.
                   1257

Yankee Doodle

Yankee doodle went to town,
a-riding on a pony
stuck a feather in his hat,
and called it macaroni.

Yankee doodle, keep it up,
yankee doodle dandy
mind the music and the step,
and with the girls be handy!

Father and I went down to camp,
along with Captain Gooding
and there we saw the men and boys,
as thick as hasty pudding.

Yankee doodle, keep it up,
yankee doodle dandy
mind the music and the step,
and with the girls be handy!

And there we see a swamping gun,
large as a log of maple
upon a duced little cart,
a load for father's cattle.

Yankee doodle, keep it up,
yankee doodle dandy
mind the music and the step,
and with the girls be handy!

And every time they shoot it off,
it takes a horn of powder
it makes a noise like father's gun,
only a nation louder.

Yankee doodle, keep it up,
yankee doodle dandy
mind the music and the step,
and with the girls be handy!

__ __ __ __ __ __ __ __ __ __   __ __ __ __ __ __ __ __ __ __

314   1141
1322   1911
843   337
1163   337
1762   2323
112   121
423   3263
423   915
3222   1813
1141   1184

Answer: Cornwallis surrenders

Crack The Code

The pig pen code, below, was a spy code used during the Revolutionary War.

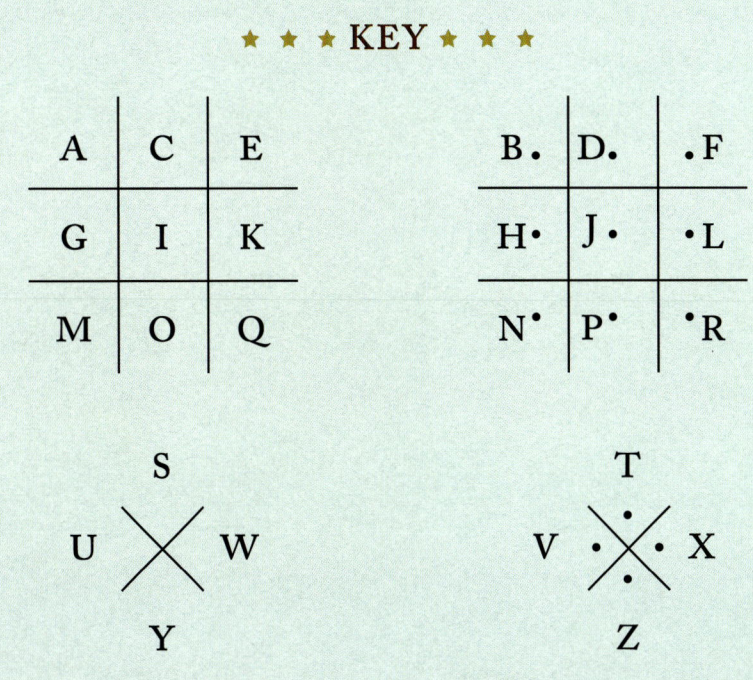

★ ★ ★ KEY ★ ★ ★

To discover the message below, find the right line and dot combination in the key above, and then write the corresponding letter on the line below it.

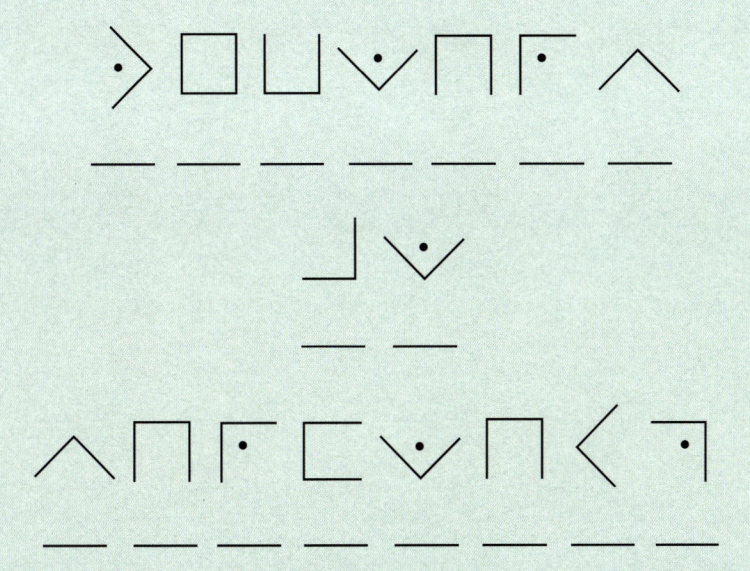

Answer: Victory at Yorktown

American Revolution Museum at Yorktown ✦ 47

Gift Shop

The Gift Shop features period reproductions, educational toys and games, books, gifts, souvenirs and Virginia-made snacks and sweets.

Café

The Café offers a varied menu including salads, sandwiches, soups, pizza, beverages and desserts. Open seasonally, indoor and outdoor seating is available.